AF229878

LANDMARKS IN THE SAND

BY

JEANNIE CARLSON

ACKNOWLEDGEMENTS

First and foremost I need to thank my good husband, Tim for his unwavering support that made this book possible.

Thanks to Jen MacMillen of Greater Good Media for taking a chance on first publishing my poem-photo combos in the *Northeast Journal* (www.northeastjournal.org), leading to the compilation of this collection of poetry.

Thanks to everyone on the St. Pete Press team who helped make this book a reality. Special thanks go to Amy Cianci, my favorite Engagement Director for her skill and dedication that contributed to the success of this project.

Thanks to E. Cox for contributing the photo of her special Persian cat, Sofia to illustrate my "Caged" poem.

Love and thanks to my son, Phil, my parents, Ruth and Lloyd, and all my family, including those who came before and during my lifetime as well as those who will come after.

Soli Deo Gloria

AUTHOR'S NOTES

St. Petersburg, Florida has been my home for more than half my life now. It is where, as a single parent, I raised my son, and where, as a divorcee, I met and married my husband. It's where I was a caregiver for my grandfather as well as both my parents, and it is where I gently laid them to rest.

My relationship with St. Petersburg is a love story. There is definitely whimsy at play, but I see the object of my affection clearly rather than through a haze of blinding sunshine. The landscape is simultaneously real and surreal, yet always recognizable no matter how subjective and symbolic my perception gets.

Sometimes the photo came first, sometimes the poem, but the city was my muse, consistently at the heart of my inspiration. Place and space regularly stir my imagination. It is where a story starts for me.

"Setting the Table for Your Story" is a creative writing video I made for Keep St. Pete Lit that explains this further. Visit

keepstpetelit.org/online-writing-courses-2/setting-the-table-for-your-story

The author would like to

dedicate this book to

T.B.

CONTENTS

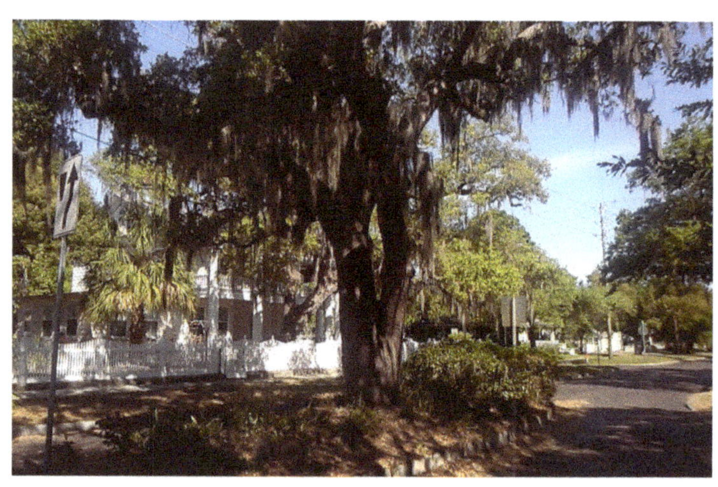

SPANISH MOSS

An old woman is praying
With glowing sunlight blurring
Her verdant countenance of indistinguishable features;
Face upturned to heaven,
Her grayish corkscrew hair
Rapunzels downward
Brushed by waving zephyrs
As she sits naked and still
With withered arms
Embracing her oak legs
Tightly tucked to the solid trunk of her
Deeply weathered body.
Bare bark exposes
Wrinkles and wisdom -
A statue and testimony
To creative life,
She implores God
For the renewal of the
Strength and beauty
Already bestowed upon her

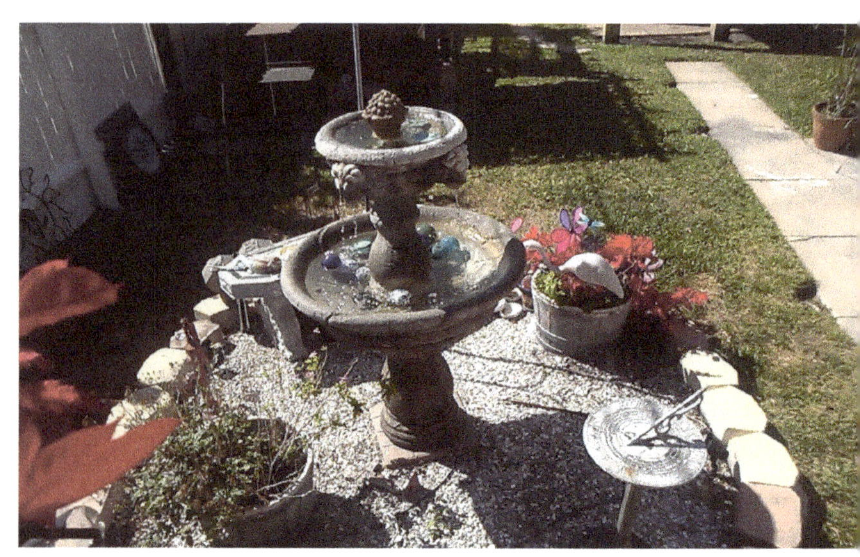

ODE TO THE GARDEN FOUNTAIN

What new spring is born and reborn? Is there a new burst of
liquid beneath the earth?
At last wondrous Walden's Pond empties forth, epic and natural,
Streaming and squirting, teeming and churning
The blue gold that sallies up two tiers and drops tears down
That quenches the thirst of humanity even when they do not
Know that they are thirsty,
The water that sources and outsources all life,
Refresh and recycle, keep rushing,
Absolving, purifying, baptizing, sanctifying,
Nurturing, irrigating, satiating, extinguishing,
Fortifying resolve and renewal to move with nature's tongue,
To listen, glisten and reflect upon your generosity
Wet in the concrete container for all to imbibe,
Dynamic in density, compelled to leap in the air
And return to the bubbling basin, a swirling emergent well.

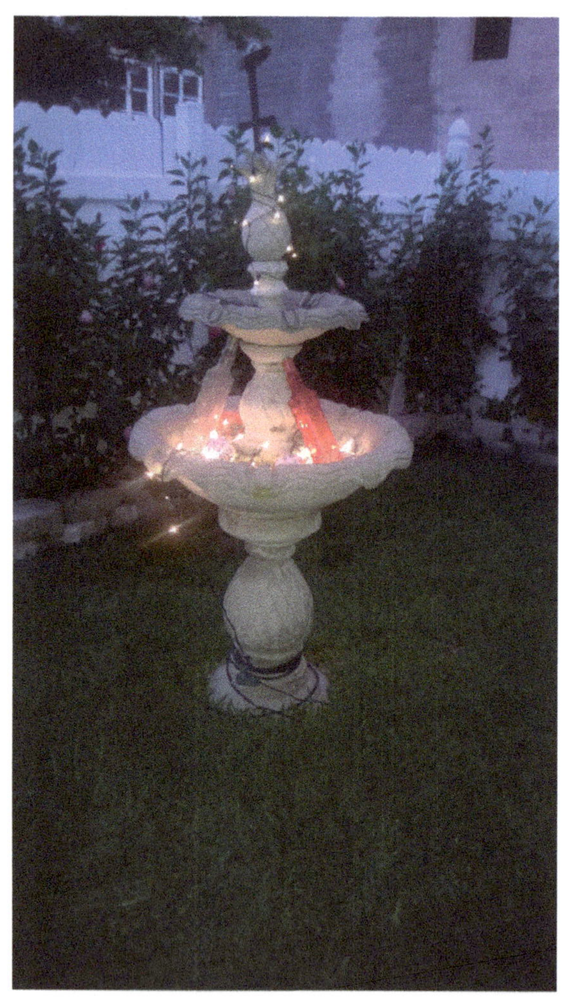

FIREFLIES

My dreams are filled with fireflies
Dynamiting the darkness -
Neon neurons navigate,
Shimmering and shimmying,
Flashing a coincidence of memories -
Glowworms consume me
With their bioluminescence that
I want to capture in cold crystal jars
(Without lids),
Lapping wet diamonds
Churning the past,
Pinging against the glass enclosure,
Trapped and saved at the same time
From growing dim

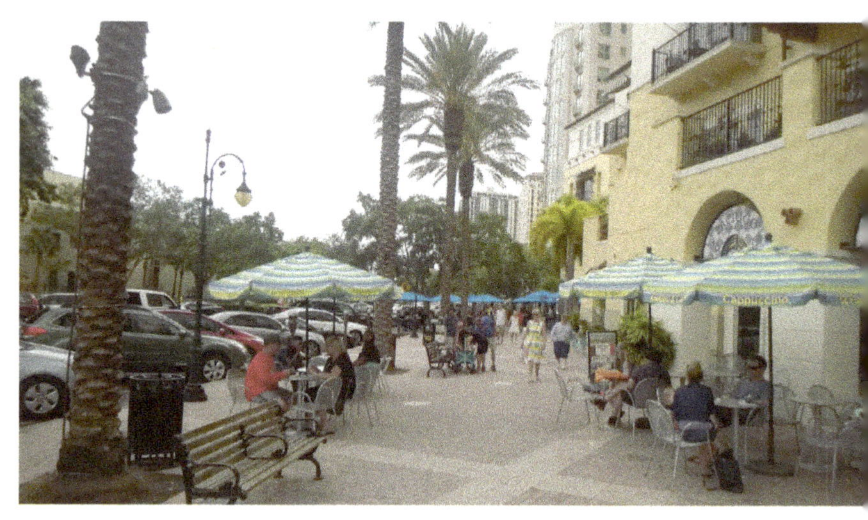

Landmarks in the Sand

DOWNTOWN SUMMER

Sweet heat still
Pacing in a contiguous line
    Downtown
Across from the Museum
    Of Fine Arts
Across from the married
    Banyan trees
Further across from
    The Vinoy basin
    The Vinoy hotel
        Pink and luscious
Like a swelling reflective wave

Sweet heat still
Aggressive squirrels demanding nuts
    Yours or theirs -
Three horse-drawn carriages
    Empty but driven
    Driven but empty
Clopping coping cuddling

Sweet heat still
Blinders keeping on track
    I know their names
    Whisper their names
    Touch their manes
Like a swelling reflective wave
And walk on home
Sweet heat still

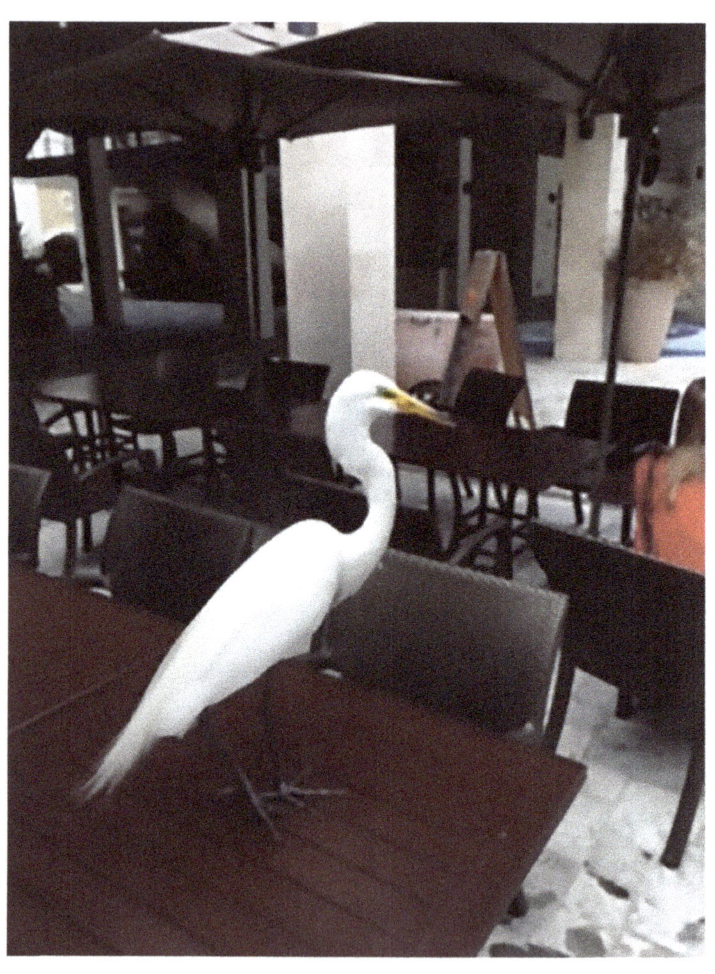

Landmarks in the Sand

EGRET ON A TABLE

Uninvited
Intrusive
Spread like a stork
About to proclaim
A new arrival

Lying in wait
Foraging for fries
Fishing for a feast
Imposing on picnics
Pestering patrons

Attracting a waiter
To shew him away

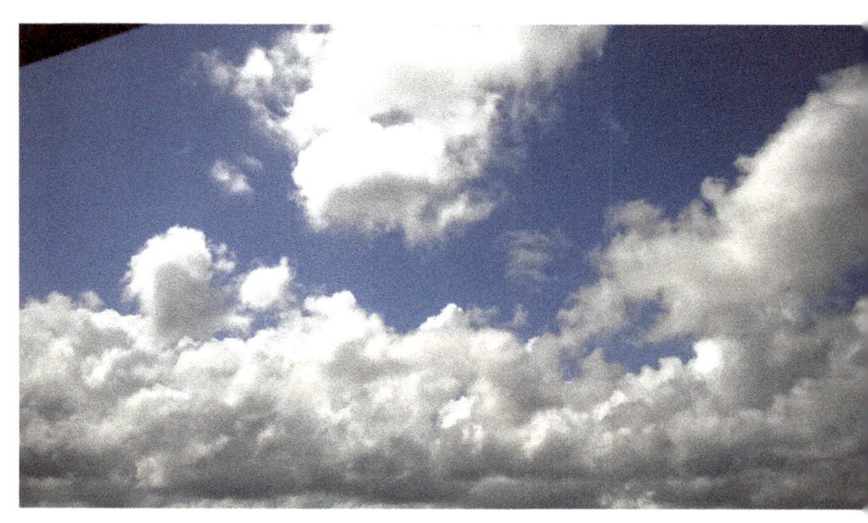

Landmarks in the Sand

OVERCAST

Obscure clouds try
To block the light, but
Not for long -
Gray on white streaks of squiggles
Brushing past the blue felt -
Shredded dirty Q-tips stick on
Poodle fluff blowing by
Wagging its tail
Tipping its fedora
Feigning deference to the Divine
That always lusters through
Polishing patinas
Making mortals look up

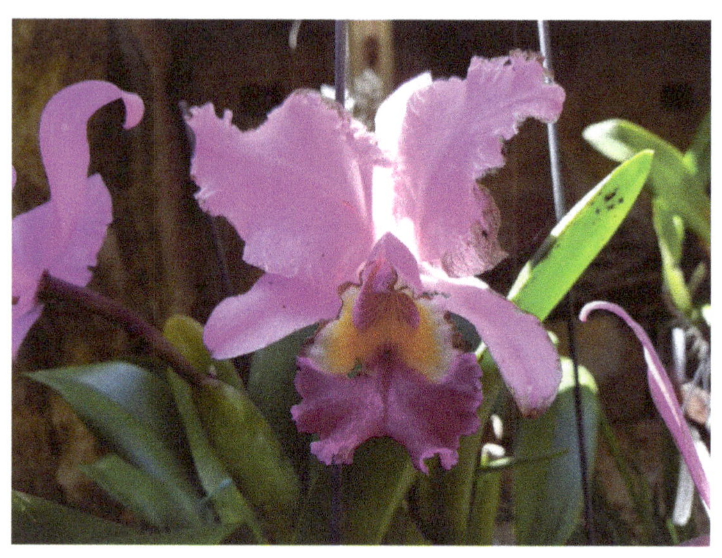

WEDDING OF THE PURPLE ORCHID QUEEN

Elegant
Undercurrents of refinement
Resonate
With the innocence of wildflowers
As a true queen
Presides over the blossom kingdom
Subjects bowing to her
Royalty
Loyalty
Gliding to matrimony
Glowing in the gilt
Dignity of the gracious
Garden gift
Corsages on the ground
Boutonnieres
On life's lapel ~
With outstretched arms
Golden tongue
Bouffant coiffure poof
Capped with a winged tiara

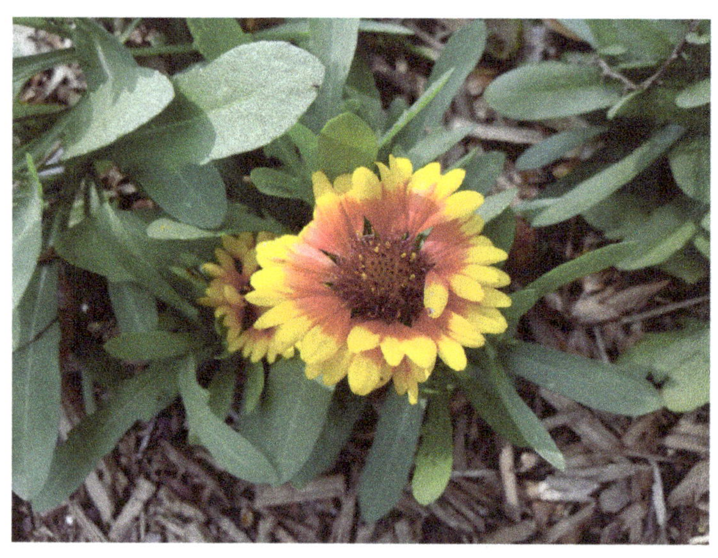

Landmarks in the Sand

SINGLE LADY BUD

Sun-striped curls and
Full blush
Centered on
Amethyst stardust
Eye shadow
Donning a forest
Green tunic
Dancing a bouquet
Expressing
Immanent transcendence
The fragrance of creation
Odor and ardor
Combine to call
A ring on it

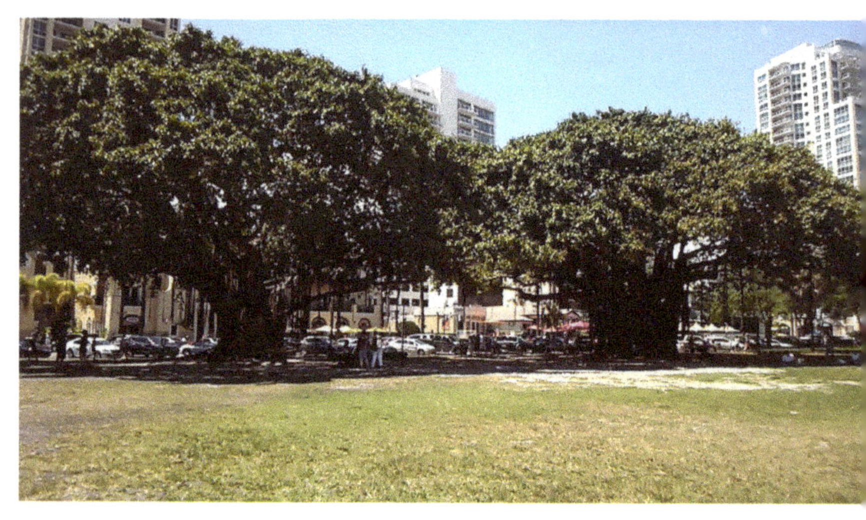

Landmarks in the Sand

BANYAN SOULMATES
BY THE VINOY BASIN

Once twin seedlings deployed by a bird in flight
Landed upon dual unsuspecting hosts,
Each enthralled with the view of the other,
Now destined to titillating transformation -
Constant needy branches reach out to be nourished,
Embracing life and love,
Shedding what used to be the self,
Absorbing the liquid thoughts between them,
Resurrecting and rooting,
Seeking the supple soil below -
Trunks develop and thicken downward,
Fostering figs and fusing as they cross each other,
Languishing in a lustful latticework -
Producing a thick and shady grove,
The copulating couple grows together over time
To ultimately emanate as one ~

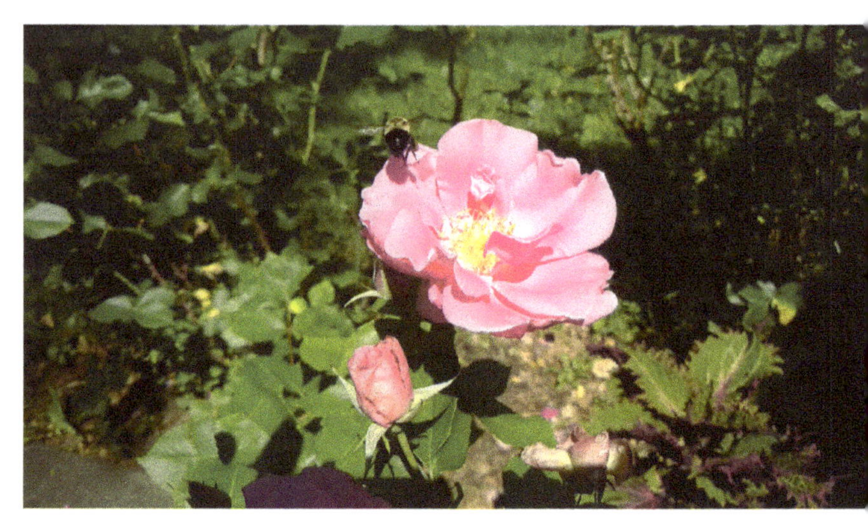

Landmarks in the Sand

ENCOUNTER WITH A BEE

Curious bee lands 3.2 on the back of my cradling hand,
The bee locked eyes, all those multi-mirrored optics,
Undivided attention all around;
He bestowed a butterfly kiss,
Fascination like a one-night stand,
No fear, no anger, no threat;
Hovering like a helicopter,
Not the blossom he expected,
Still he left a memory on my pillow ~

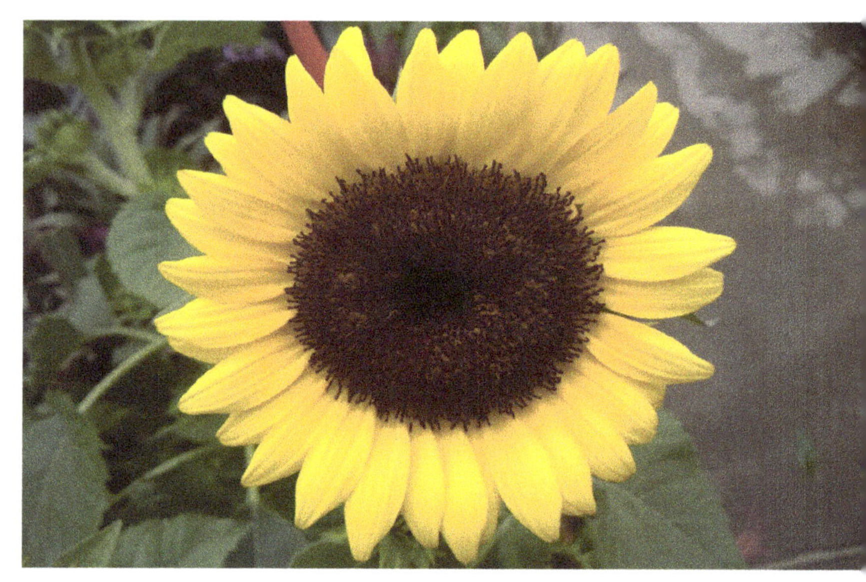

Landmarks in the Sand

SUNFLOWER

Adulterated sprout
In a topiary full of unexpected glory,
Uninvited longevity and loyalty penetrated
The center of the inviting void;
Mathematically perfect polar coordinates
Pitch Vogel's pattern, a spiral cluster of florets
Packing efficiency in the flower head, divining head,
Spewing successive Fibonacci
Undulating in full gilded glaring, fondling,
Stiffening, releasing, repeating -
Holy wholly unforbidden oil, seeds, butter,
Life perpetuating

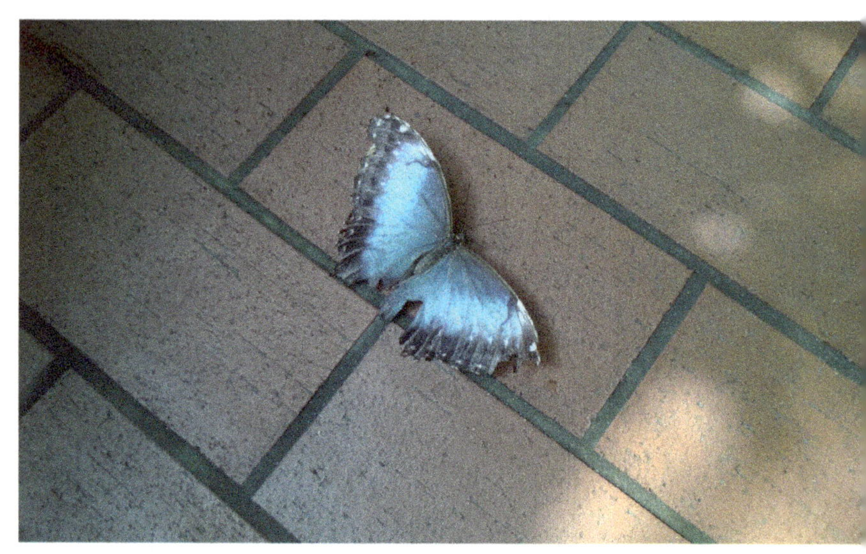

Landmarks in the Sand

A GARDEN SONNET

A blue butterfly scampers across the landscape,
Three trees left, two trees right,
Shadowing a path of lawn between, around, before and after,
One decadent daisy fully opened,
Fallen leaves, dried and inanimate,
Scattered like the dust they will become;
A fence delineates fields not in use,
Chain links format a garden,
There to grow nature and to keep nature out
All at once;
What's being cultivated, I don't know,
Containers for garbage, compost, water
Not catching everything
People less.

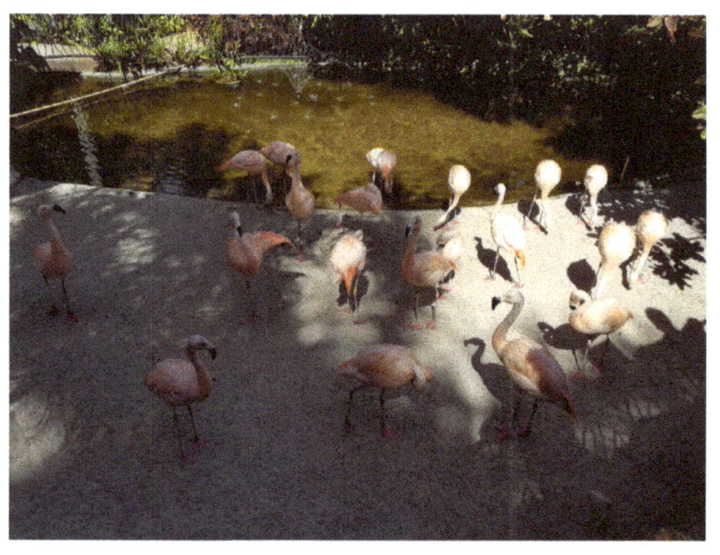

SUNKEN GARDENS FLAMINGO CONFERENCE

Clustered together in glorious weather
Getting their feet wet and well met
Preening feathers in the pink of a blink
Ready, set – go get
Dithered druthers –
Hors d'oeuvres of cat food shrimp and salmon pâté
More to be noticed than noticing
Jockeying for position
Each in the way of the other –
   Mother, brother
       Bother father
          Farther garner
Fake intent
Honking intermittent
Bursts of belated admonishment –
   Astonishment

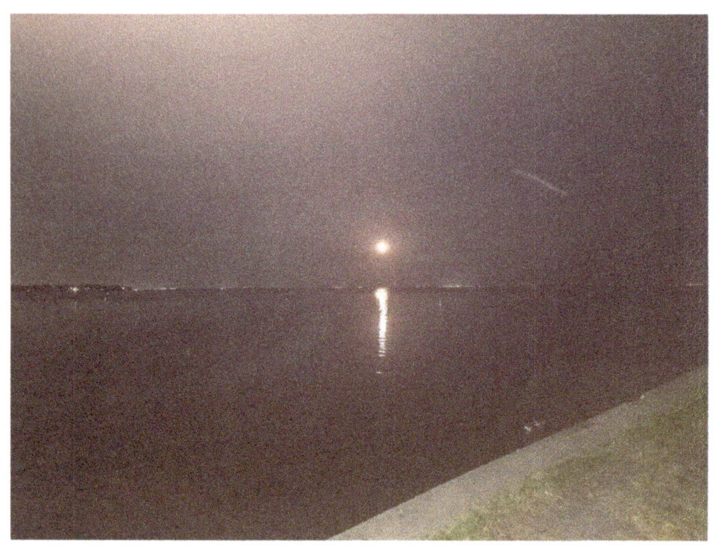

Landmarks in the Sand

MOON OVER NORTH SHORE PARK

Misty autumn moon
Blurred by billow
Checking its reflection in the bay —
Anyway, let's say to see who is the
Fairest
   Fullest
       Favored
Jousting with the waves
Clamoring against the
Dodgy dowdy cloudy night
Brushing against swaying silver cylinders
If the angle is just right for accord —
In fractious diva
Dimensions of deciduousness
Scores the flawless high note —
Solidarity of a solo soprano

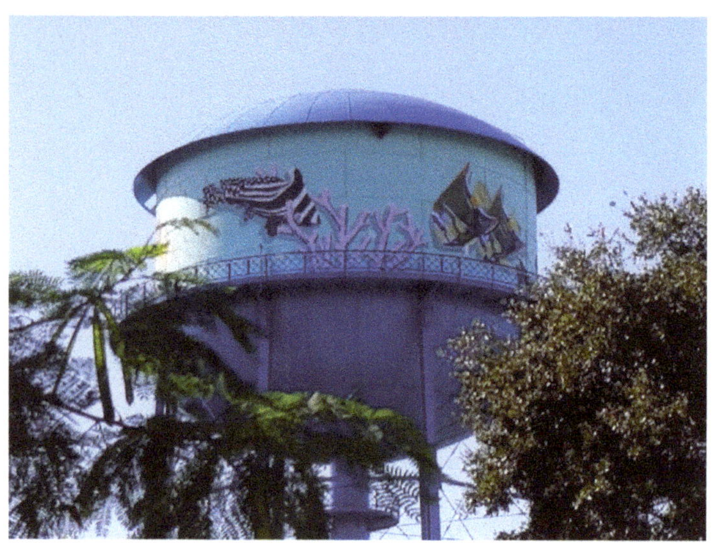

Landmarks in the Sand

WATER TOWER AQUARIUM

Swimming in paint
Looping
Around and around
In an unending sphere
Carousel clear
Playing a silent disc
Overlooking Crescent Lake
Here a ring of tropical color
Fins chasing one another
Circling higher than birds flying—
Stagnant fizz bubbles
Frozen in brine
Foundering equidistant
From freedom and the sublime
Fading in time—
A clique of seasoned sea emoji
Held aloft
By sturdy metal feet—
An offering
Without tartar sauce

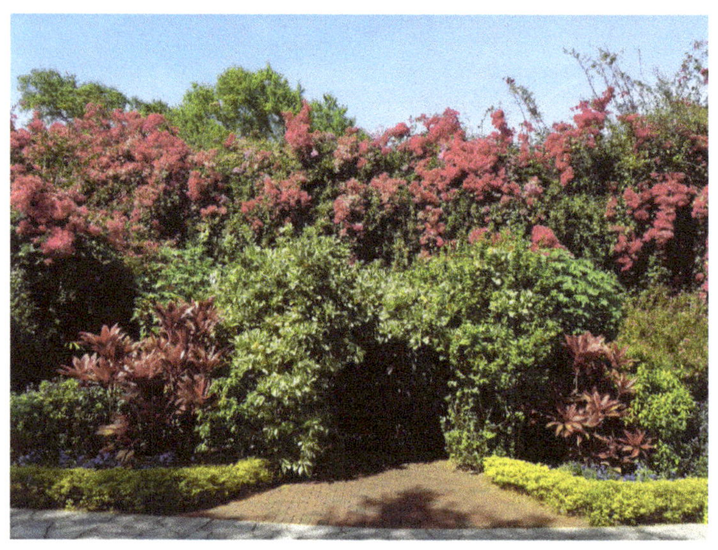

SUNKEN GARDENS GROTTO

Alive with time
Transporting through nature
Where green is life and
Life is luxury;
Loving is literal
Mindfulness in mysterious thoughts to
Synchronous relevance
Spiritually aware of the universe,
A retreat from the mundane
An alcove of tranquility in the
Recess of doubled down dimensions
Hollowed out of nature and artifice
Molded in the intersection —
Past — Present — Future
Ornamental and devotional
Shrine to Saint Petersburg
Where every pilgrim is Bernadette
Attesting to the Divine ~

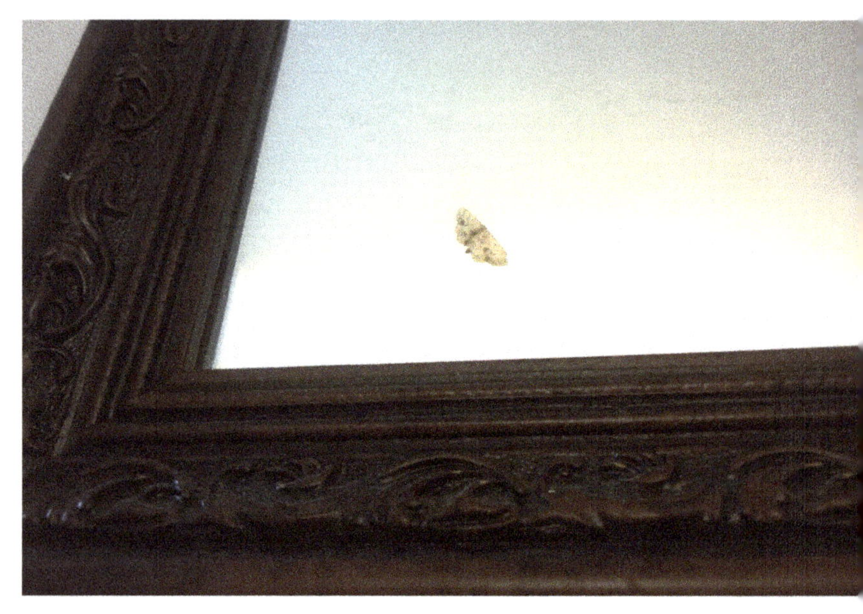

Landmarks in the Sand

MOTH LIGHT

She landed on a mirror
Mirror on the wall
And found love
In all its delicacies
In all its obfuscations
Funneled flat
Into a single dimension
Denying all its imperfections
Denying all its dangers
Sticking to the ultrasonic glass
Until paralyzed
By the miracle of a rainbow

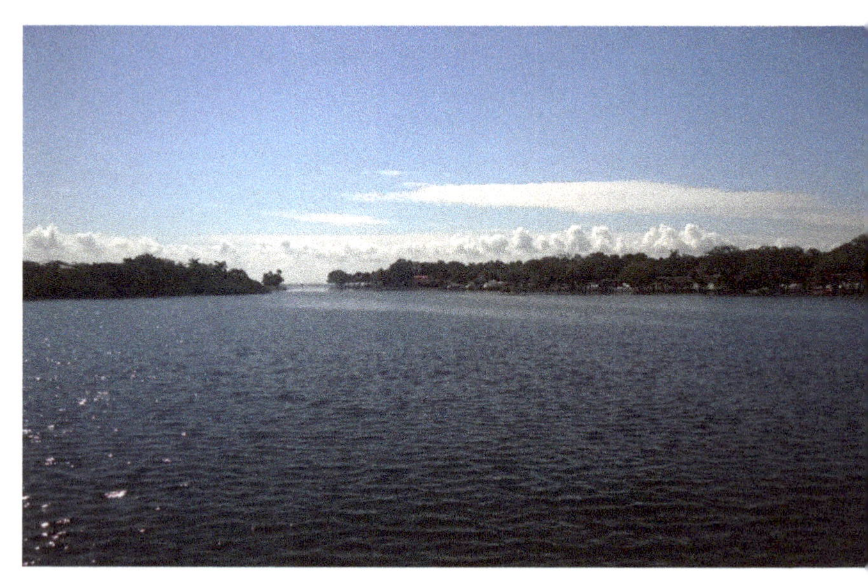

Landmarks in the Sand

CHANTEY

A voice in the water
Like Morse code
Casting the whiff of a lure
Hooting out a mystery
Tattling on the seawall
In perfect pitch
In enigma sonar
Signal flags flying
Sprinkling hints
Revealing nothing
Designing everything
In the depths
In the shallows
Moving with the current
Singing in Braille
Licking a bottled ship
Cueing a chorus of bobbing diamonds
A glissando of rushing rhythms and rippling grace

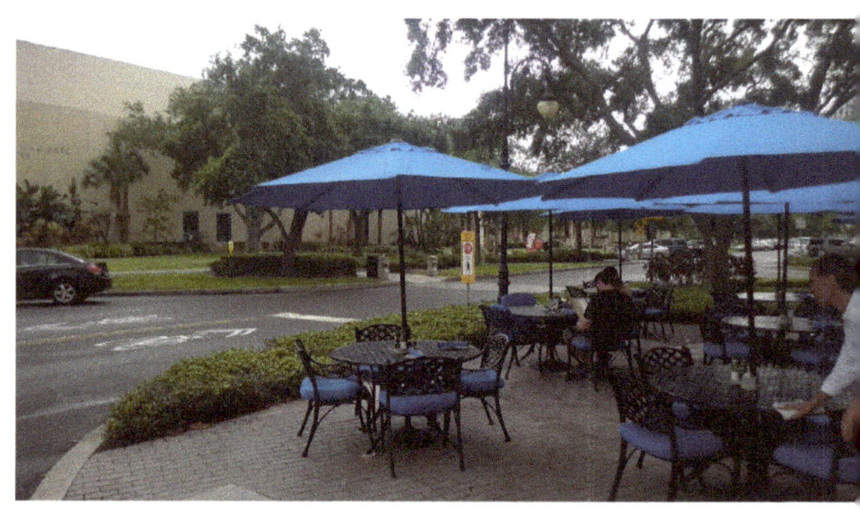

IMPRESSIONISM

Out of focus
Nature is born
Suckling flat myopic vistas -
Farsighted clarity comes...
As air is actually apprehended,
Dabs of color cohere.
Shading expands the eye's realm —
A moment captured...
The retina of a rippling lake
Reflects the face of heaven

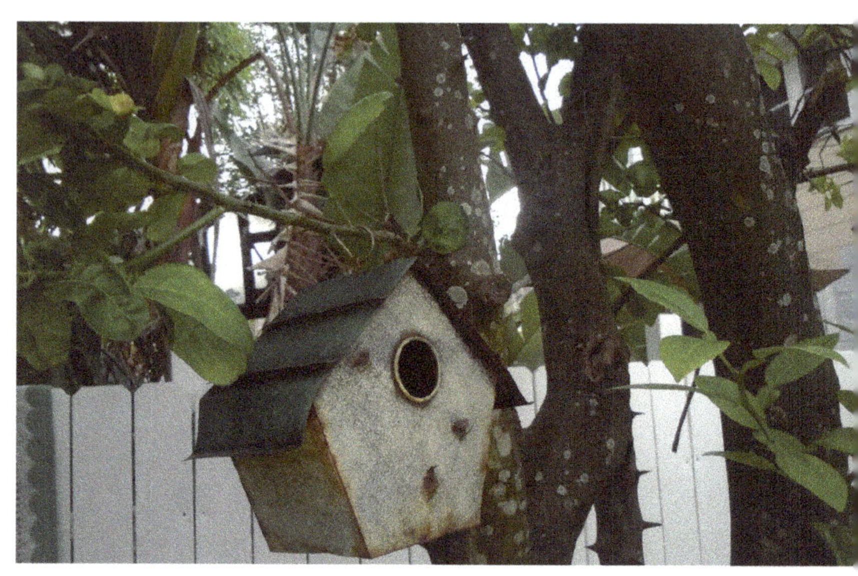

Landmarks in the Sand

DEATH OF AN ORANGE TREE

Remnant of an ancient orange grove,
You were the centerpiece of my land.
The strong scent of your blossoms
Blows in the memory of my nostrils -
The sweet taste of your palatable fruit
Puckers only a thought away from my tongue -
The shade of your embracing arms
Sways in the shadows of my mind -
The laughter and liquid
You inspired linger on -
The earth that nurtured you
Now reclaims you.
The sunlight looks for you
And shines on
The transparent apparition
Where you are rooted
In eternity

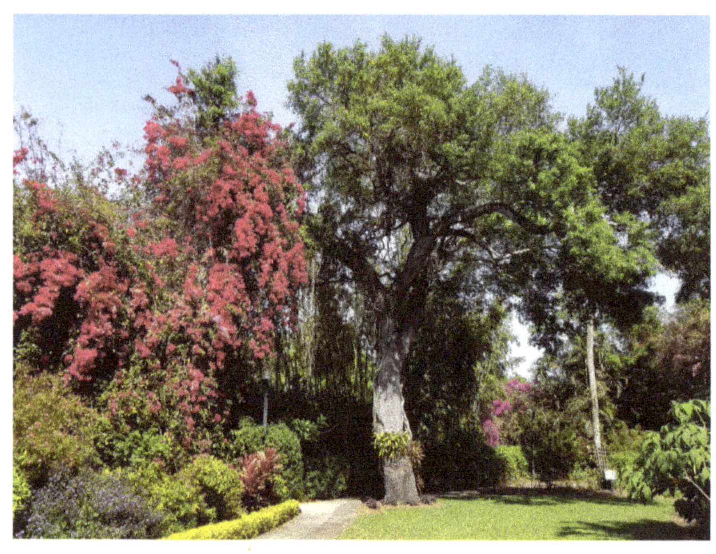

TREE CARRYING A BASKET OF LIFE

Pink accents ornament her
Shy bowed head
Veiled in grace
And vegetarian lace
Cradling a cluster
Of air plants
Bundled in a
Blessing of oneness
As nature consecrates
The infant,
A scion of earth's presents ~
Her willowy stance
Billowy blows
A verdant sea
Satiating smolder
Into her sphere ~
Molten Madonna

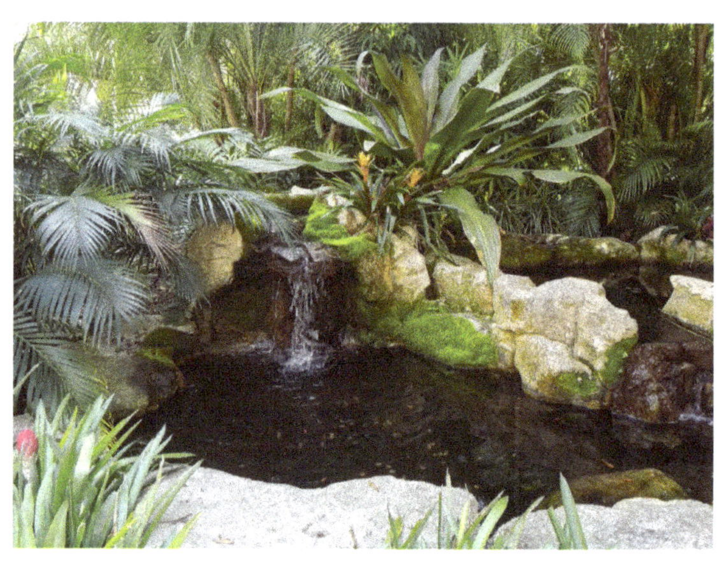

Landmarks in the Sand

SUNKEN GARDENS
FAIRY WATERFALL

Waterfall of wishing
Fairy-falls door décor
To a secret
   Sprouting space
Behind the bending braid
Mini palm fronds
And magical moss ~
Surly orchids
   Cascading
        Coolly
          Down
   Tingling ~
Delicately designed
Rock and pebble gardens
Scatter deciduous bits
For tiny trolls
To explore

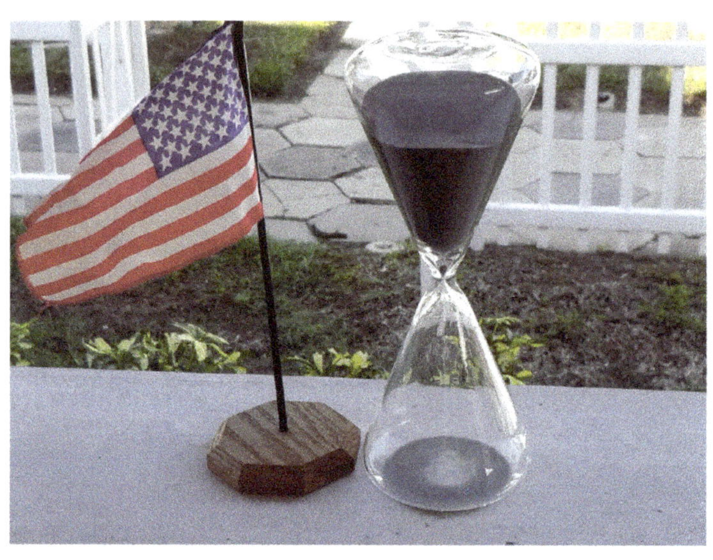

COINCIDENCE IN TIME:
A VETERAN'S DAY TRIBUTE

WORLD WAR I
Red nail polish is being dabbed on my nails
By a woman whose grandfather served with mine
    In France
    In the Army Corps of Engineers
    In the echo of a century
She showed me a black and white picture
Both men are looking at us from the gloss
    I remember in my DNA
    She sends it to me digitally
    Together we are divinely connected

WORLD WAR II
Elderly husband and wife snowbirds slip and fall
    simultaneously after the benediction
My husband and I serendipitously snatch them from either
    side
    Saving the precious couple from a synchronous spill
    But not us from their gratitude
They insist on treating us to lunch
The husband was on the battleship USS Alabama
My father was on the light cruiser USS Miami
    Both in Halsey's Third Fleet in the South Pacific
    Both on anti-aircraft guns
    Both saving each other

The sands move on and circle back again

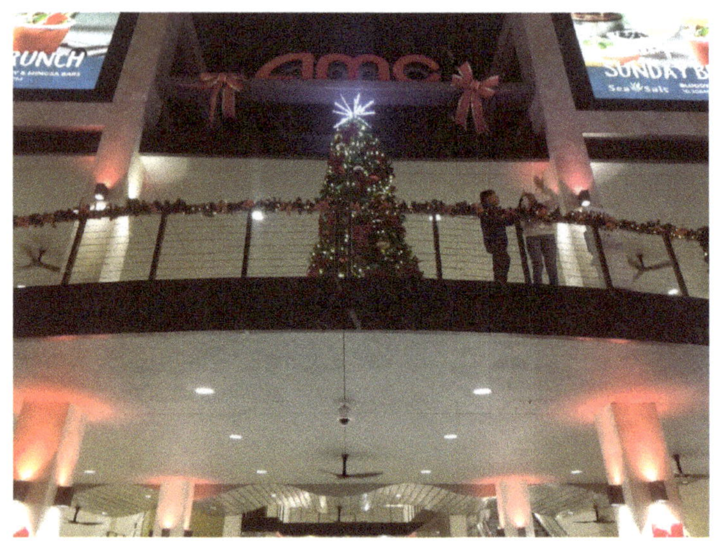

Landmarks in the Sand

SUNDIAL CHRISTMAS

Glistening tree from the balcony
Overlooks the shadow of a gnomon
Or could that be a gnome on
Pointing to pinpoint the hour
Upon a cylindrical surface
An instrument of time curious—
In all its waves luxurious
Where the date remains the same
Shining, perpendicular to the horizon
That meets the hopeful Savior
Clashing with the retail game
As dolphins leap and call His name—
Before they scurry in the frozen floodplain
Sculptures mired and admired.

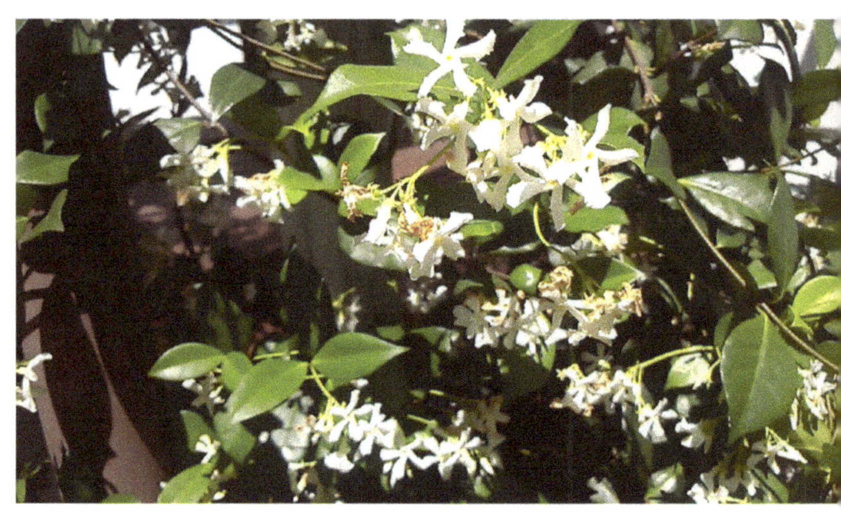

CONFEDERATE JASMINE NOCTURNE

Pinwheels plow rows of fragrance into the enchanted opening night.
Spinning starbursts cling to an arbor engulfed in garden secrets,
Subtly scenting and sweetening the tepid evening air.
Standing out against the backdrop of a purple sky,
The clambers cluster in a limited engagement.
Dreamy bud aromas waft on a spring stage
Permeating from cloistered ingénues
Costumed in the mysticism of virginal white,
As thespians fleetingly enjoying a dual-month run -
Once satiated with a season's heated nights of applause,
The eloquent bouquet bows behind the evergreen curtain
Of tangled stems that continue to
Perennially reach for the stars.

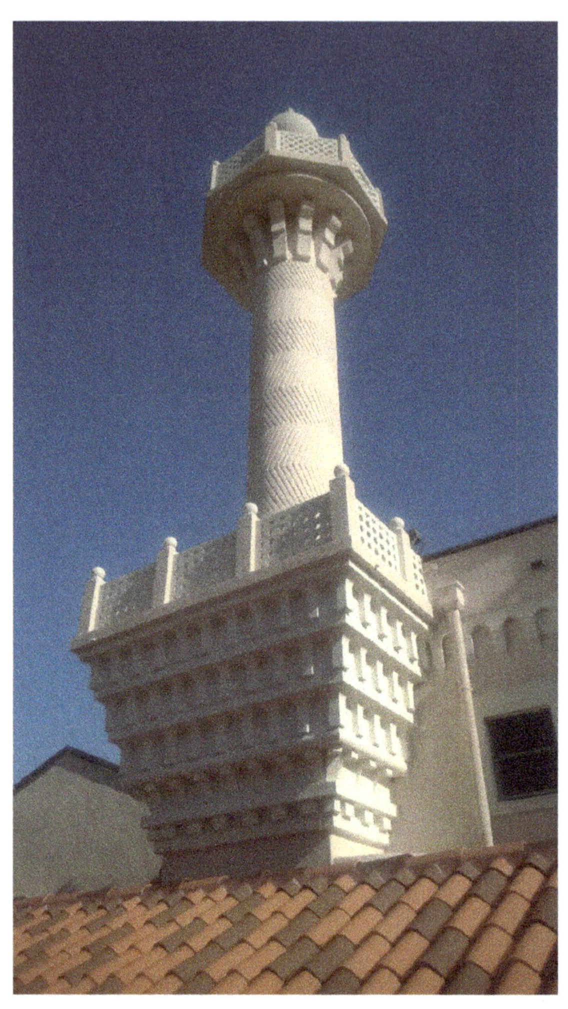

Landmarks in the Sand

THE IVORY TOWER

Below us
A leprous world
Infects rainbows,
Draining the color
With indifferent bloodlessness
Until only the achromatic dregs
Distort a once prismatic sky.

Immune up here...
The precipice of their infirmity
Cannot contaminate
Unrestrained imaginations -
Unlimited ethereality
Shields and sustains
Our visionary scheme ~

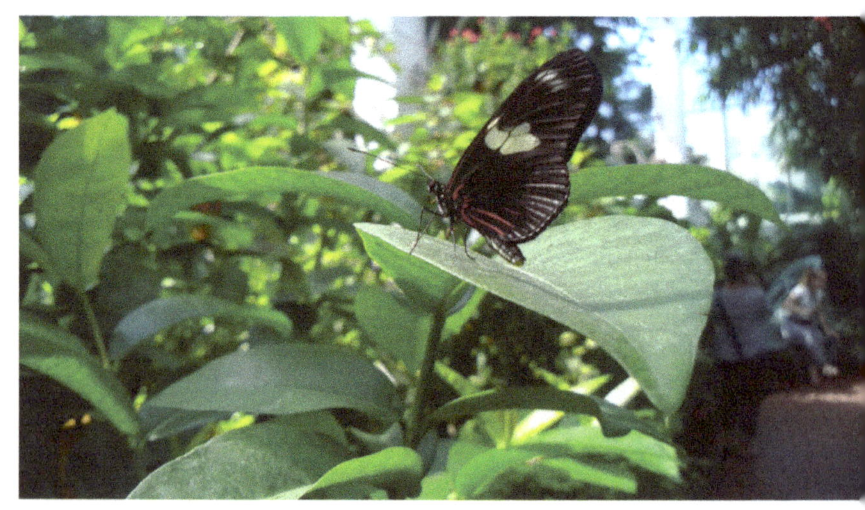

Landmarks in the Sand

WINGS

Camouflaged
Holding a lorgnette
Alert antennae
Streaks
Of rouge
On her fuselage
Is saturated with
Reflective flora –
The leaf dips
In admiration
From the weight
Of awe
As the throne
Of angels
Acts in Atlas unison
Elevating thread-like legs
In support
Of rapture

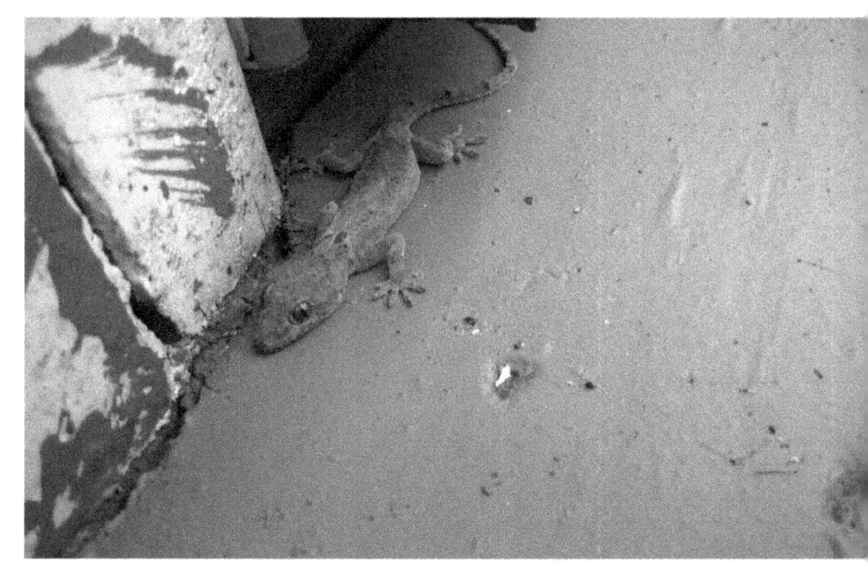

Landmarks in the Sand

HIBERNATING LIZARD

Cold against the cracking pavement
Stopped in his tracks
Flung frozen in quantum calculations -
Eyes wide shut as slits
Fingers spread surprised
Elbows arched in arthritic lock
Perplexed, pallid, paused
Stuck in sneaky snowless Florida winter,
A gray ghost embarrassing himself anemic
Caught half-undressed
Mid-shedding and anticipating
Another season of forward momentum,
Color, calm, collusion with nature -
Springing into resurrection
Exposing a universal hue

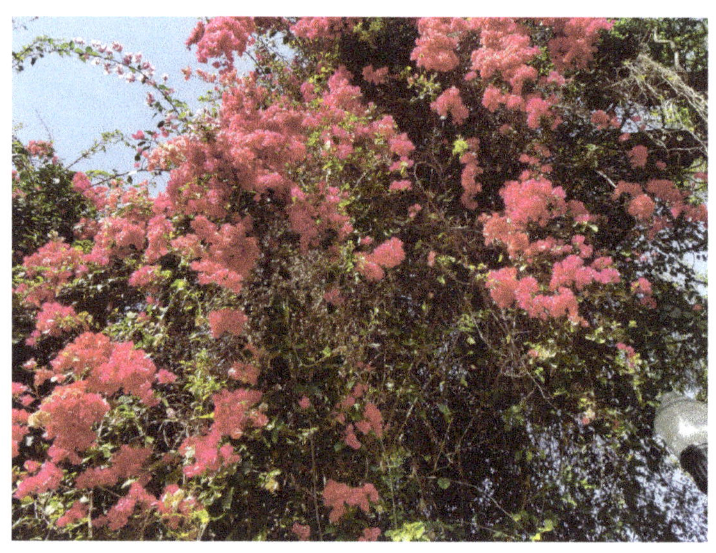

PINK AVALANCHE

Powder of pink
Flowing like instinct
In the flower fall
From the heights
Entraining insights
Onto the unsuspecting
Below,
A natural hazard
Of a lovelorn storm
Layering affection
As they go
Binding those
In the way
Of nature's flux,
Gasping for breath
And grounding
In the flower-slide's
Overwhelming aroma

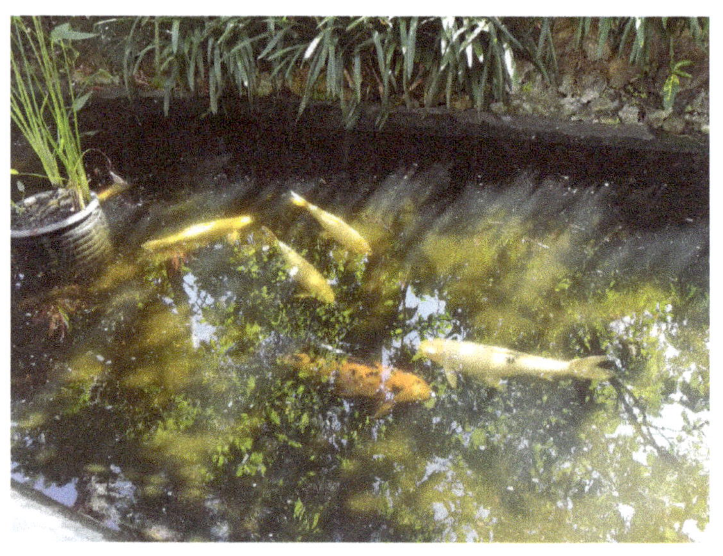

Landmarks in the Sand

CARP/E DIEM

Enlightened
Frolicking
Naked
Fish
Reflecting gold
Good luck
Acting koi
Isolated in a peaking pond
Neither predator
Nor prey
Just seizing the day
And swimming away
Meditating on the lily pads
Muse of the leaf ridden mire

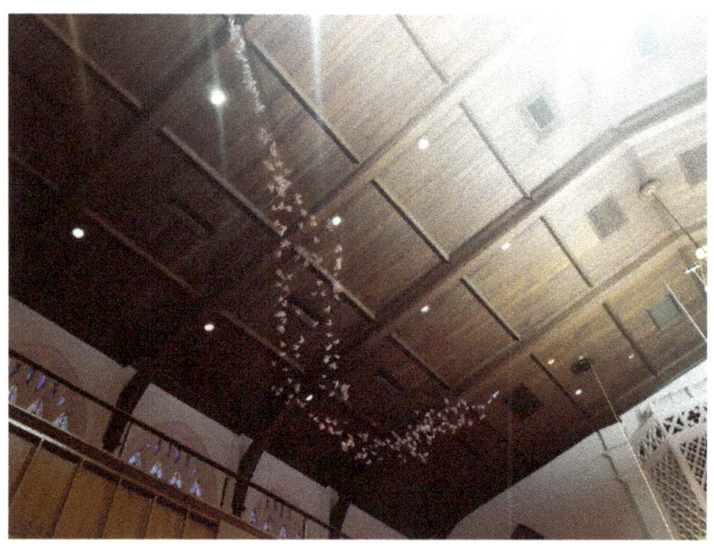

Landmarks in the Sand

ORIGAMI DOVES

Flying high among the holy mahogany rafters
Diving and weaving
Following and pursuing
Determined to carry divine entreaties
Prayers on pointed wings
Instinctively stringing the flock
Circling back
To the universal source of authority
With the power of words and the Word
Folded with a prize in the center
Offering peace
Without making a sound

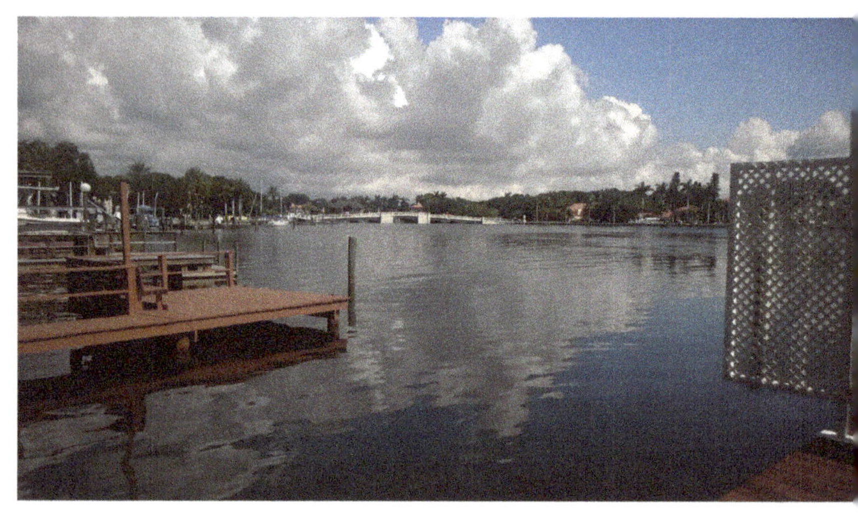

Landmarks in the Sand

INTERMITTENT

Bridges are impermanent connections
Reaching beyond ordained potential
Brighter overhead than at either destination
Longer and shorter spans depending on the trip
To the past or the present
With just a tinge of the future
To the familiarity of the unknown
And the exhilaration of erratic exploits
Crossing over concrete
Leaping over liquid barriers
To touch the sporadic sea fog
Blowing into twin clusters of clouds both ways
Conjoining the living in a natural state
Of momentum and acceptance
With the hesitation of afterlife

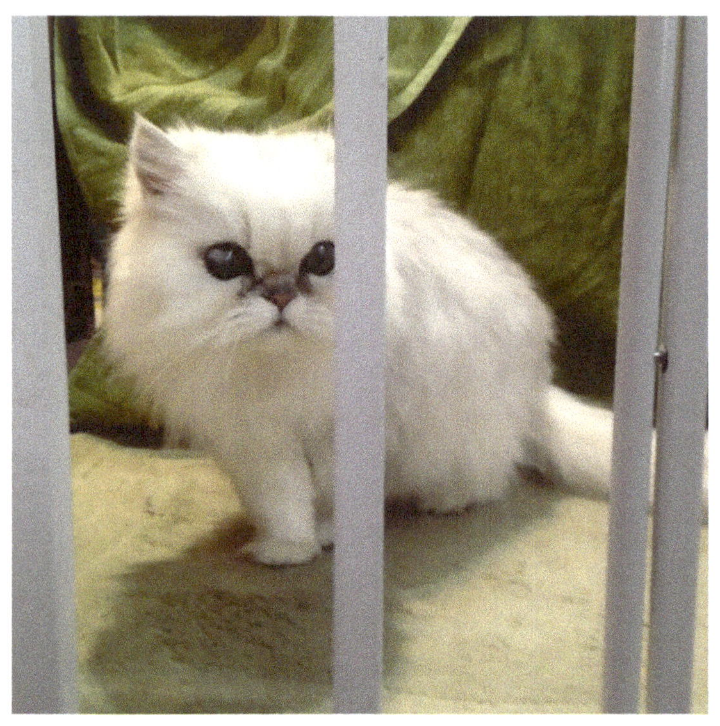

          Landmarks in the Sand

CAGED

Soullessly a sleek and sinewy
Striped cat stalks
Too small a cage -
She paces proud protuberant paws
The space of her confinement -
Resigned not to a fettered fate,
Felinity is ever ready
To pounce ferociously to freedom -
Clawing a crevice,
Only her whisker
Can claim bristly visit
The incalculable void -
Undaunted, the direct
But stoic semiprecious eyes
Seductively suggest
One dare approach -
Either to set her free
Or be devoured ~

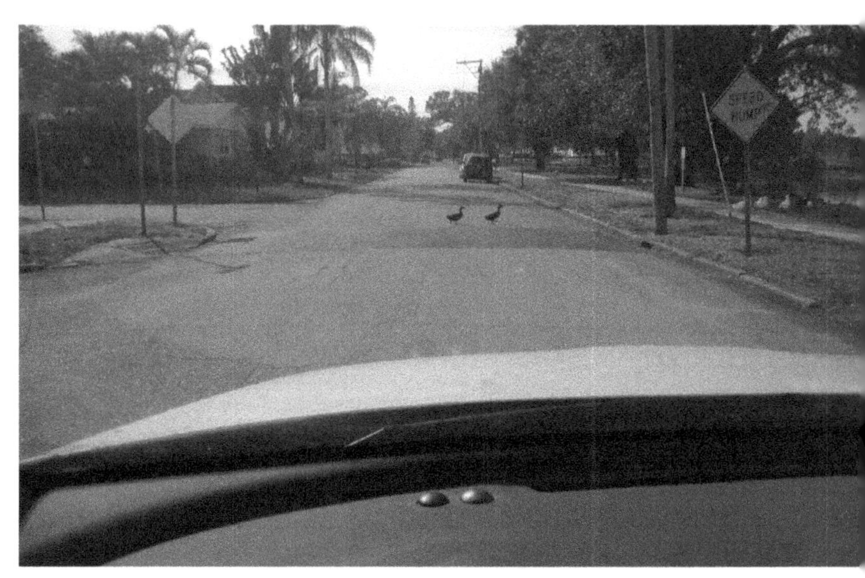

Landmarks in the Sand

DUCKS IN THE CROSSWALK
AT CRESCENT LAKE

Dashing ducks in sterling string
Winging their way
As gentleman beau
Beaks bowing braced
To the likely ladies
In waiting white
In gleaming ground
For the flash of a rendezvous =
Waterfowl curtsy lakeside
Ruffled feather fans finery
Plump pump across
Staying between the languid lines
In priggish procession
In proprietary pecking order
To make a match =
Stopping traffic
The Muscovy way
Of anticipating a team
Beyond the badling
   To the paddling
   To the flocking
Leaving behind the speed hump sign

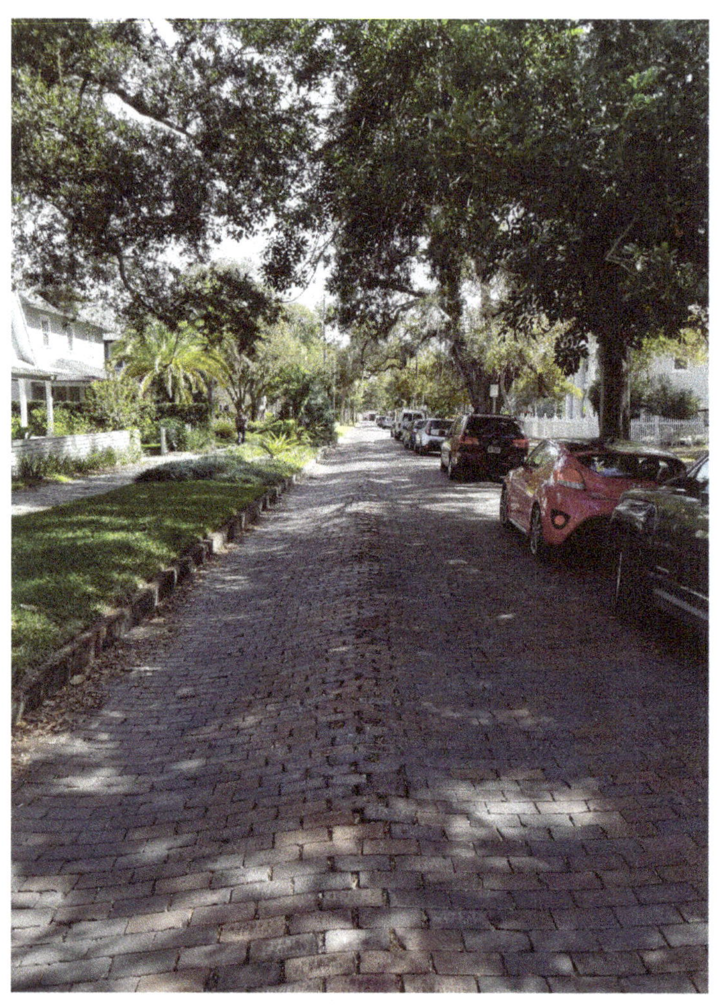

Landmarks in the Sand

OLD NORTHEAST BRICKS

Pebbles piled like memories
Rocks rolled away from the tomb
Reverberate
Bricks that bind
Stones that speak
Pedestrian pathways
Construct tomorrow
Step backwards
Build now
Sink and sway
Gnawed into grooves
By water and weight
Unmerciful wheels of thawing time
Alluring alleys with secrets to survey
In the cornered crunchy consistent clay
That retains rectangles in a circular slippery sense of momentum

Crossroads mimic a consternation of decisions
Incisions
Lots of legs two four and many more
Walk trot crawl run gallop drive and sometimes fall
Pieces of every neighbor soak in
All roads lead to home

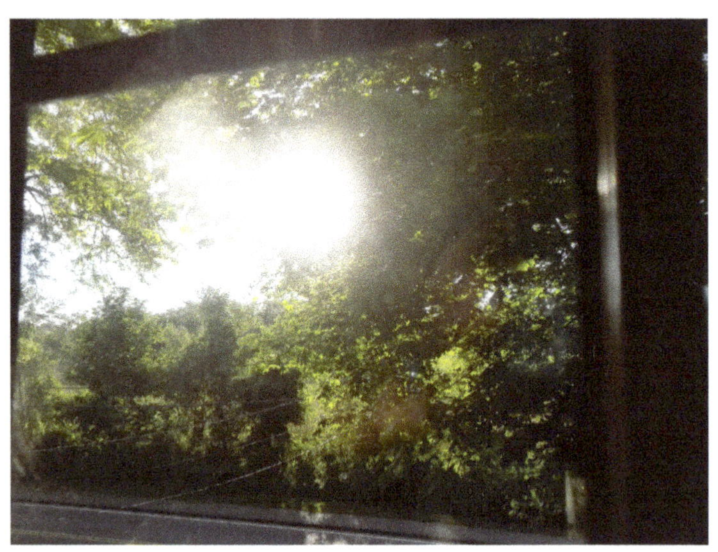

Landmarks in the Sand

DAWN'S GRACE

Sun squints code
Through the trees into an eastward
Facing window with flashes of illumination
Each light break sears a new take
Into the pupil of the soul that
Bares it whole and holy in refracted will –
Even wobbly glass of the past
Enhances magnification –
Deep diamonds cut through
Sleeping lids in rhythmic slits until the bits
Cannot be denied, just adored –
Chandelier in the sky
Harmonizing with the birds in the backyard
Like the first day of creation
Catch the flame, the leaves –
Prying open a peculiar cascade of olive fusion ~

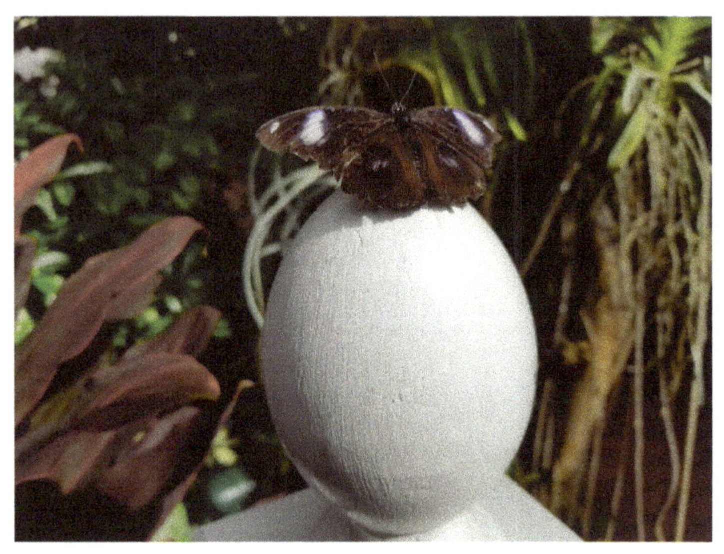

BUTTERFLY ON AN EGG

Drab brown butterfly that could pass for a closet moth
Stands on an egg way too large for her to claim as her pupa
Yet she claims it just the same
Proudly dancing a jig on the gigantic shell
Her spindly tiptoes tapping a pantomime magical
From which an ostrich could sprout --
She doesn't know what is within,
Just what is without --
Joy and life everywhere --
She is madly maternal
Clapping her wings
Thinking of soft motherly things
Insisting in her own way to stay
To see it through and true
Until the Eternal laughs out loud --
His breath blew ----
    her from her perch.

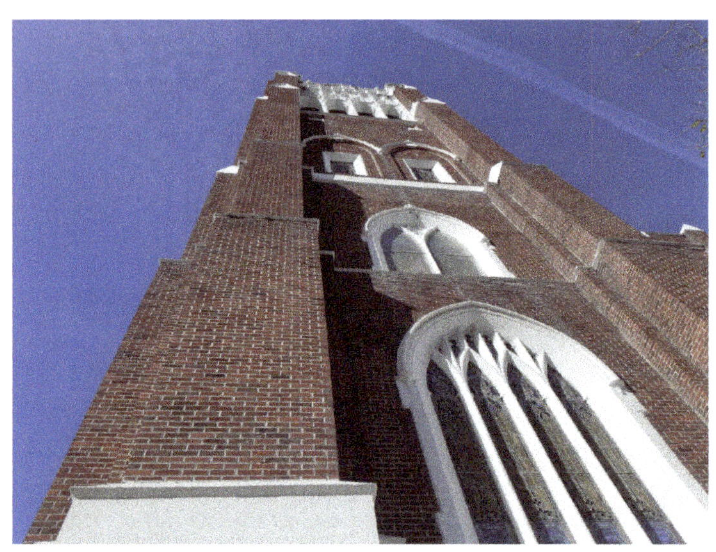

Landmarks in the Sand

BELL TOWER THURSDAY

(In gratitude to St. Mary's Catholic Church and St. Petersburg
   First United Methodist Church for playing their bells Thurs-
   days at 2pm in support of healthcare workers)

Ring, ring the bells
   Chimes that dispel
Thankfulness decibels
   Therapeutic Thursday knells

Ring, ring the bells
   Let the air swell
With resonating prayer
   Lifting angels everywhere

Ring, ring the bells
   Whose pealing quells –
And arches a jet stream
   Akin to rainbow beams

Ring, ring the bells
   Where Hope dwells
Tolling Mercy, Kindness wells
   Again, ring, ring the bells!

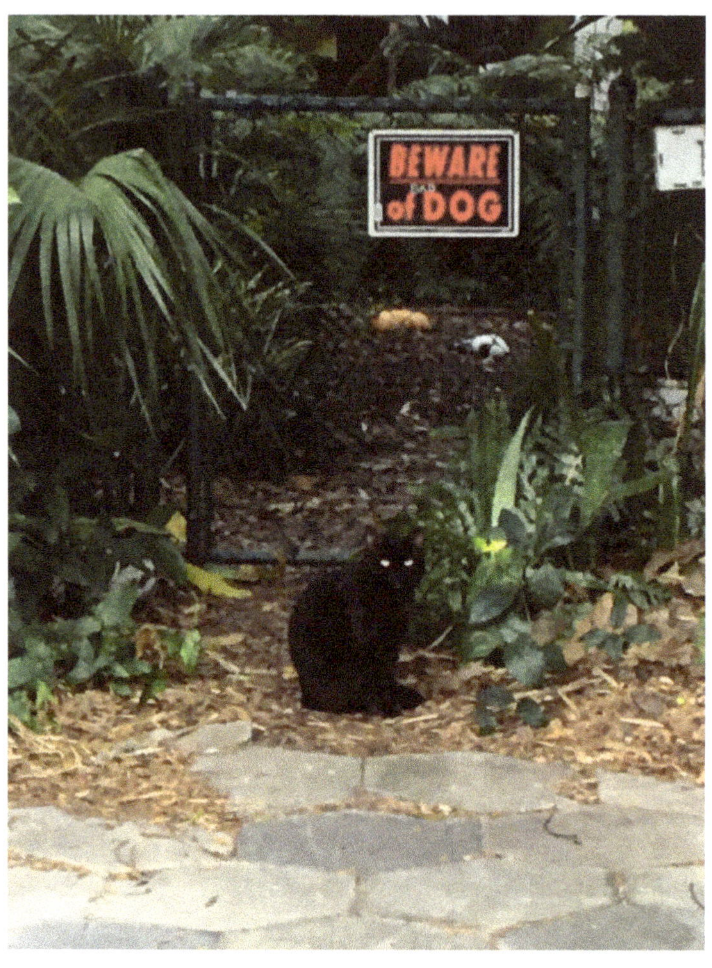

Landmarks in the Sand

CATTITUDE

Raw verisimilitude
Irresistible pulchritude
Not to be shooed
Or come unglued

Unlimited latitude
Bellowing beatitude
Devoid of decrepitude
Systematically shrewd

With voice meowed,
"Not happening, dude!"

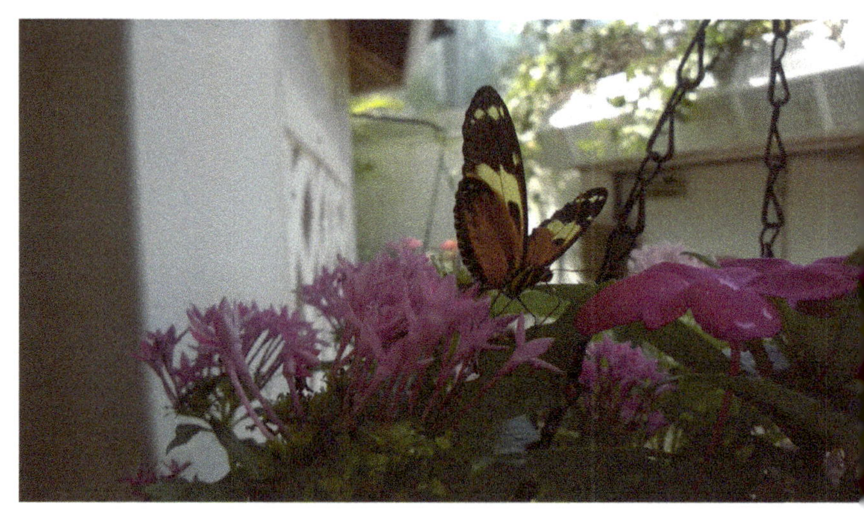

METAMORPHIC TREASURE

Yellow luscious letters
With the emotion encapsulated
Still...Suddenly
Released from the attic box cocoon
Take flight in a flurry —
Fringed in sepia symmetry,
Touching and tickling,
Triumphant over the tempest of time;
Their tone is succulent,
Sublime, vibrant -
Wistful wings flutter,
Tantalizingly,
Overwhelming me with
A silent serenade
Glistening on my essence -
Succumbing to the resonating sweetness,
I salivate at the supernaturally
Eloquent memento of you ~

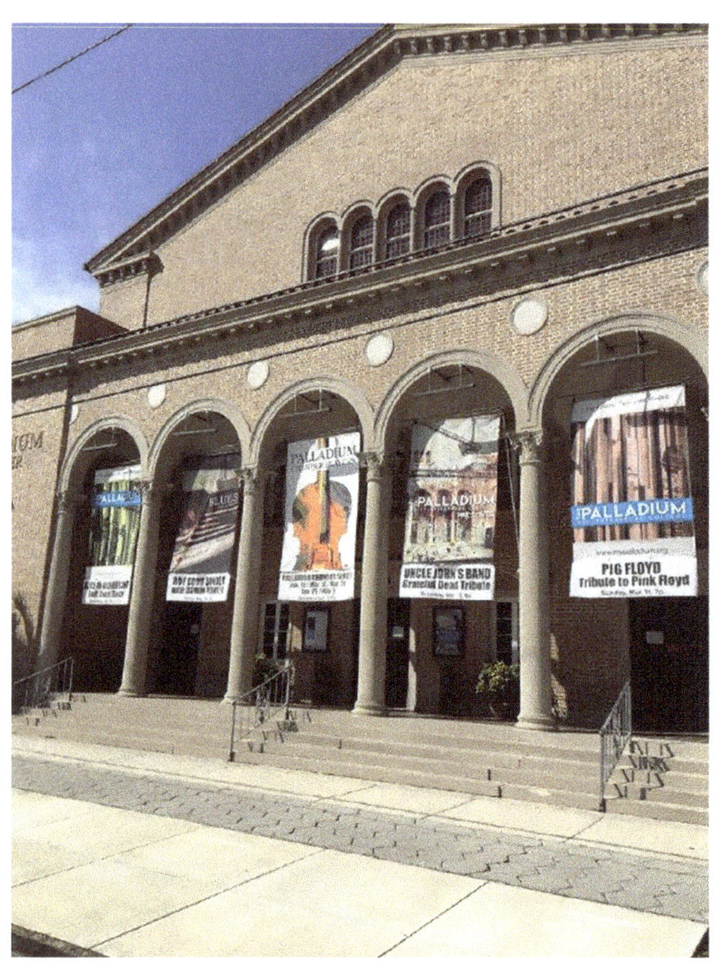

Landmarks in the Sand

VIOLIN

Mellow sounding seasoned box of wood
Lies against a virtuoso's shoulder
Breathless -
Singing pianissimo
As the bow strokes her,
Melodies emerge Stradivariously -
Sentimental strains
Sweep the strings
To a pitch of frequency
Orchestrated
With an underlying tone
Musically passionate,
Soulfully colored and darkened.
The plucky lady draws admirers
But responds
Only to his touch ~

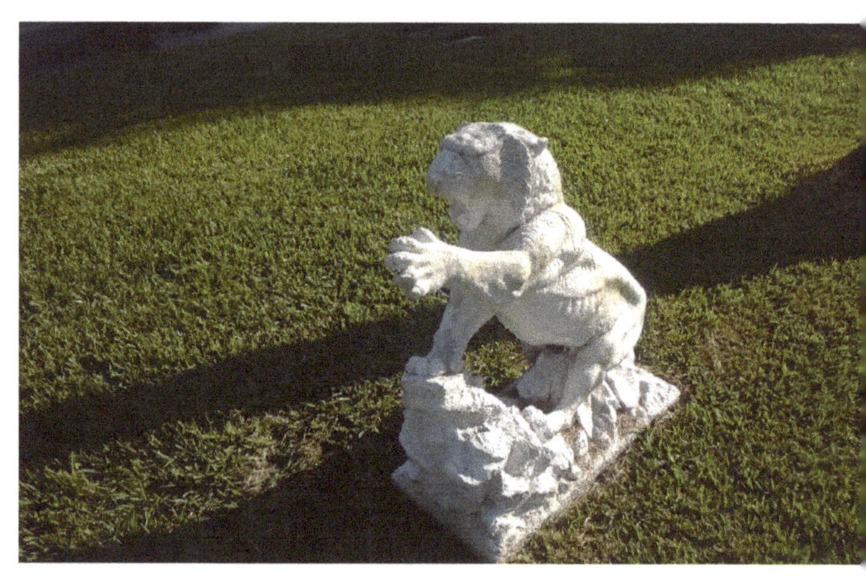

Landmarks in the Sand

PANTHER STATUES ON SNELL ISLE

Bleached stone panther each
Mired in purity blocks
Clinging to a ghost of a litter box
Stretches out
Without getting out
Markers of mission
Save a Polaroid purpose
Scampering in stasis
Alternately purring and preening
Voicelessly
Preparing to pounce
Growl hiss or roar
Negotiating the neighborhood
In invisible prowling prowess

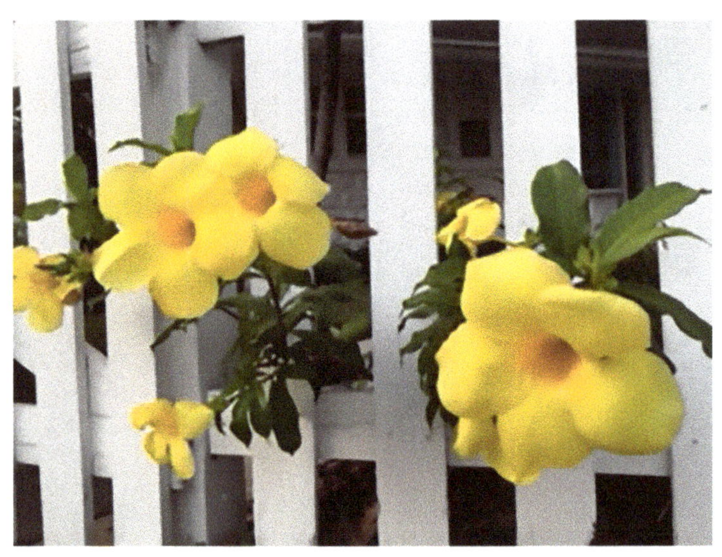

Landmarks in the Sand

YELLOW FLOWERS THROUGH A FENCE

Flower children faces
Lodged between the slabs
Smeared like senap mustard
Beautiful as butterflies
Dangerous as yellow jackets
Pure sepia singing punitive parodies
Jailed in wistful white wood
Gold as a baby's tousled hair
Flung back in a loud laugh
Satisfied to see the sun
Citrine bright and muted
Calm as chamomile tea
Crowned in bejeweled canaries
Bemoaning prissy petals free
Upright as an upstanding yield sign
Alerting a summer sunrise

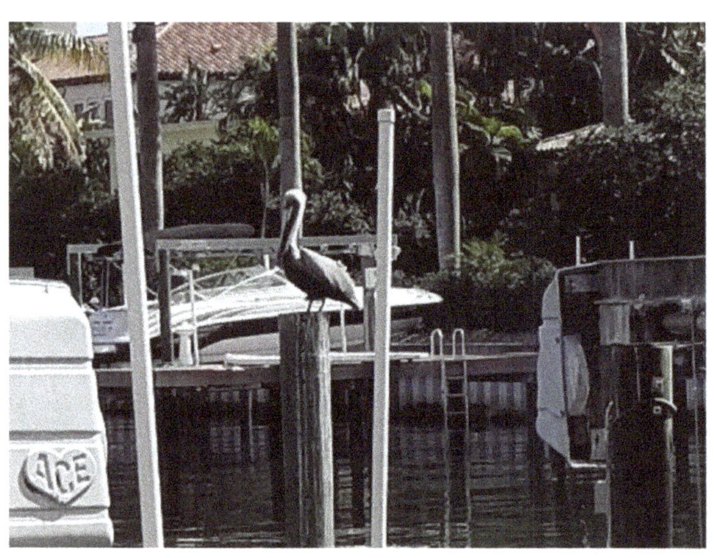

Landmarks in the Sand

PELICAN POLE DANCER

Deep white demure feathers
Costumed in innocent grace
Provocative and pure
Profiling her pouch pouting face
Checking out all the wiggling fish
Watching from below
Desires in tow
Esteeming her as they go
Or so it would seem
Pausing in the water like a dream
Believing they are in charge
When they are not
She is
The one with the power
To wave them on
Or consume them
In their own fluids
Wet and wondering

ABOUT THE AUTHOR

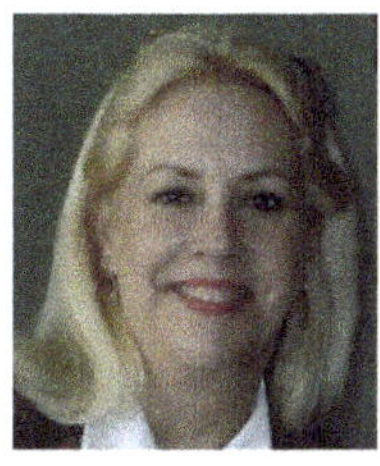

Jeannie Carlson is an award-winning writer experienced in fiction and nonfiction genres, with multiple freelance credits, published in newspapers, periodicals and books internationally. She has a bachelor's degree in theatre from Randolph-Macon Woman's College, Lynchburg, Virginia and a Master of Fine Arts in Creative Writing from Naropa University, Boulder, Colorado.

Born in the Scandinavian neighborhood of Bay Ridge in Brooklyn, New York, Jeannie grew up in the New York metropolitan area where she sang in professional theatre and opera. She is a NYC transplant, but considers herself a semi-native of St. Petersburg, Florida where she lives with her husband and their chatty housecat.

Jeannie is a correspondent for Tampa Bay Newspapers, Inc. as seen in *Tampa Bay Times*, TBNWeekly.com and *Beach Beacon* among others. She has taught English and English Literature courses at St. Petersburg College and Hillsborough Community College. A contributing writer for the *Northeast Journal*, Jeannie pens a bi-monthly poetry column, ONE Inspires where the results of her wandering the neighborhood come to fruition.

Visit her at *www.JeannieCarlson.com*.

www.ingramcontent.com/pod-product-compliance
Lightning Source LLC
Chambersburg PA
CBHW050010040726
47599CB00014B/1312